IF WE WERE STARTING
OUR MARRIAGE AGAIN

If We Were Starting Our Marriage Again

John & Betty Drescher

ABINGDON PRESS

Nashville

IF WE WERE STARTING OUR MARRIAGE AGAIN

Library of Congress in Publication Data

DRESCHER, JOHN M.
  If we were starting our marriage again.
  1. Marriage—Religious aspects—Christianity
  2. Drescher, John M. 3. Drescher, Betty, 1928–.
  I. Drescher, Betty, 1928– . Title.

  BV835.D74   1985   248.4   84-14444

ISBN 0-687-18672-2

Scripture quotations noted RSV are from the Revised Standard Version of the Bible, copyrighted 1946, 1952, and 1971 by the Division of Christian Education, National Council of the Churches of Christ in the U.S.A., and are used by permission.

Scripture quotations noted NIV are from the Holy Bible: New International Version. Copyright © 1978 by the International Bible Society. Used by permission of Zondervan Bible Publishers.

MANUFACTURED BY THE PARTHENON PRESS AT
NASHVILLE, TENNESSEE, UNITED STATES OF AMERICA

CONTENTS

To our married children,
who were much in our thoughts
as we wrote these chapters

PREFACE

Once upon a time there was a wise and respected religious teacher walking along the side of a cliff. He stepped upon an unsteady stone which sent him sailing through the air and down the side of the cliff. He was saved from certain death when he saw a slender branch of a tree reaching out from the side of the cliff and grasped it with his teeth.

As he hung there one of his young disciples appeared at the top of the cliff. The disciple stood in deep thought for a few moments and then asked: "Tell me, O Master, what is the meaning of life?"

This seems like a suitable story to begin a book about marriage. There is real danger in our saying anything when we feel, at times, that we only are hanging on by our teeth. But no doubt that is the way every married couple sometimes feels. And it is this which humbles us when writing a book on what we would do if were were starting our marriage again.

More than any other relationship in life, marriage has the greatest possibilities of making us either better persons or bitter persons. Some, in the closeness of the marriage companionship, call from each other the best in traits, disposition, and character. Others, in the intimacy of the marriage partnership, pull from each other the worst of traits. Some, after years of marriage, grow into beautiful persons. Some, as time passes, become embittered persons.

This is true not because one marriage has more adjustments, differences, or difficulties than other marriages. There never was a marriage that could not have been a failure, because the elements of disharmony are present in every marriage. Marriage fails when we do not work together in a caring way. We develop the best in each other when we express daily appreciation and seek the good of each other.

In looking back over the thirty years of our married life we agreed on a number of things. While at times we may have doubted our love, we agreed that if we were to begin again we would choose each other. The longer we live together, the more we see how much we need each other and why we were attracted to each other.

Then too, as we review the past, we see where we have changed. In some things we improved by being together for three decades. We crossed some high hurdles together and we are better for it. We were forced to face ourselves many times and, in spite of the frustration and fear this often brought, these experiences also turned into blessing. We found that difficulties can become doors to new discoveries. Differences can add dimension. And struggles stretch our marital muscles to give new strength.

As we look back we see some areas where we struggled and in which we still need to grow. Some things we did poorly. But in spite of these, we have learned to live and love together.

Best of all, as we view the past together, we see many elements which we feel are enduring ones. We want to share them in hope that someone, somewhere, will be helped. They are not meant to be a simple set of rules or a formula for guaranteed success. Sometimes we feel like Heinrich Heine, who wrote many years ago: "Here's to matrimony, the high sea for which no compass has yet been invented."

Heine's exclamation is true, because each marriage is unique even as each person is unique. Yet there are reliable guides and proven pointers which can bring happiness in every marriage. There are ingredients which will forever work, if we are dedicated and diligent enough to *make* them work. We know what follows has been tested in many marriages, and to some degree will be present in every happy marriage.

FOR LIFE

We shall walk together
in the deep security
which drives out all fear
of forsakenness,
of separation,
of lost love;
So that each step
will confirm the vows
made at the altar,
and each day
will know a deeper love
because we commit ourselves
to do and say that
which builds love
as long as life shall last.

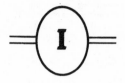

WE WOULD BUILD ON
COMMITMENT

Last summer we visited friends who were students with us during seminary days. We discussed the direction of our lives since those earlier times together, and talked about our marriages and families. John and Ellen told us that they had repeated their wedding vows to each other at least twice a week since their marriage thirty years before.

"Twice a week?" we asked.

"Yes," they said. "We memorized our vows to say to each other, so why not say them to each other more than at the wedding?" We knew of those who repeated their vows at each anniversary; but twice a week—that was new.

As we pondered John and Ellen's practice and talked about it, we think we discovered their secret of success in marriage and in life. Yes, John and Ellen no doubt had rough times, as every couple has, but it was this kind of constant commitment which helped to pull them through many of them and made the journey joyful and enduring.

Jacob and Amanda Friesen live in Mountain Lake, Minnesota. Jacob called one day, giving an invitation to visit in their home. He said, "Although you may forget me, I'll guarantee you will never forget my wife."

Jacob and Amanda were married in 1936. Several years after marriage all of Amanda's body joints were stiff from rheumatoid arthritis. She was unable to bend her body. Jacob and Amanda lived together with this condition for over forty years. She is able to see persons and read by adjusting her prism glasses. Jacob made a bed for her which uses electric power to turn a gear causing the bed to move from a horizontal to a vertical position.

During the visit Jacob and Amanda shared that it was their deep assurance that they married in the will of God and their commitment to God and to each other before and after marriage which kept their relationship strong all the years. This deep commitment helped Jacob be a happy, kind, and considerate husband, ministering to Amanda's needs. So also it was that deep commitment to God and her husband which kept Amanda a loving, happy, and gracious person who grew in character, in interest in many things and persons, and in a ministry of prayer, while her body was immovable.

That day Jake and Amanda said that they believed the missing word in much of the talk about marriage today is the word *commitment*. Out of deep commitment came all the other ingredients which have kept them strong, loving, and faithful.

Commitment, the Core

We have discussed the meaning of marriage much between ourselves and also with others in many marriage retreats and seminars. We conclude that if we were starting our marriage again we would emphasize and build on commitment even more than we have in the past. We also confess that it was our commitment to God and to each other, and our deep sense of what the permanence of marriage means, which helped pull us through difficult days and brought us to a fuller love today.

"To love someone," says Erich Fromm in *The Art of Loving*, "is not just a strong feeling. It is a decision, it is a judgment, it is a promise." We are persuaded of the permanence of marriage and of the teaching that says, "What therefore God has joined together, let not man put asunder" (Mark 10:19).

Our daughter and her husband wrote their own wedding vows. We were struck by the seriousness with which they took their commitment when they said, "We will not consider divorce as an option." We believe that to consider it as an option is to weaken marriage from the start. To consider divorce as an option is to deny the sacredness of marriage held by the Scriptures and the church.

Joseph Bayly, writing in *Eternity* magazine, says: "Somehow we must restore the sacredness of the marriage vows. Maybe there could be two different ceremonies: one for those who have forsworn divorce and remarriage; another for those who consider divorce and remarriage an option 'if it doesn't work out.' I'd like to see all the latter such ceremonies relegated to the County Clerk's Office."

In an article entitled "Build on the Dignity of Marriage," Waylon Ward says: "One of the most significant factors affecting marriage appears to be the idea that 'love' becomes the foundation couples try to build on instead of 'commitment.' Most couples' understanding of love is emotional and fickle. They fall in love, get married, fall out of love and get a divorce."

Judson and Mary Landis stress that a commitment to permanence in marriage is the only logical starting point from which a successful marriage can be built. They write in *Building a Successful Marriage* that those who marry considering divorce as possible are already steering toward divorce. Successful cooperation in marriage is impossible when limitations are set upon it. The will to succeed is motivated, many times, by the commitment to permanence.

Without this commitment, small difficulties drive persons apart. All who are married for even a few years know that no meaningful or lasting marriage can be built on the philosophy "We will live together as long as we love." Rather, marriage can last only on the commitment "We will love together as long as we live."

What greater thing is there for two human souls
Than to feel that they are joined for life—
To strengthen each other in all labor,
To rest on each other in all pain,
To be one with each other in silent, unspeakable memories
At the moment of the last parting.

—*George Eliot*

More Significant Than Problems

We now believe that the kind of commitment we make to each other is what holds our marriage together during the difficult days. If that commitment is to permanence, then it will not be superseded by financial, health, or any other problems a marriage may face. When our commitment to each other is greater than the problems, the problems can be solved. But if our commitment is weak, then even small difficulties, discouragements, and disillusionments will drive us apart. If the commitment is weak, we will not work at our problems.

Just because the going gets difficult at times does not mean the marriage is doomed. We notice that sometimes the young married, in the haze of romance and glamour, think the first quarrel has ruined their marriage. Actually, it could be the beginning of a unity achieved only by toil, tears, and talking together.

The happiest marriages, we have found, are not those with the fewest problems, but those in which the partners are committed to working at their problems together, knowing that commitment to each other is greater than any problem. We now know that every marriage has enough elements of disharmony to be a failure. But, if commitment to each other remains strong, no sickness can shake love's hold, no ill fortune can destroy love's foundation, no hard times can snuff out love's spirit and strong support, and no separation can diminish love's noble steadfastness and unswerving fidelity.

One of the best definitions of love comes from someone who has been married for many years: "Love is what you've been through together." Just as a diamond is nothing but pieces of black coal welded together at the same point under terrific pressure, deep married love is that most precious possession which increases in value each day and year of pulling and sticking together.

Love Is Commitment

We now know that love is not so much a feeling as it is a commitment to act in love, to do what love should do in each situation. When our first child was born, two years after we were married, our peaceful nights vanished. In fact, all our children awakened us once or twice a night during their first year. We got up at all hours of the night to feed our children not because it felt so good getting up at night and losing sleep, but because love led us to do it. If we wait for good feelings to demonstrate love, too often little love will be shown. We need to forget ourselves out of the concern and commitment we have to each other. When we do what love would do, we find that the feelings of love follow our actions.

We now know that a spirit of self-gratification which says, "I must be me" and asks "What is in it for me?" rather than "What can I do for you?" destroys happiness. Self-fulfillment cannot be the approach if a marriage is to be happy. Such a spirit destroys the very fabric of devotion to each other. It characterizes the adolescent, who is still searching for independence, rather than the adult, who knows the meaning and need of interdependence.

We now know that one of the best things we can give a child is a deep sense that mother and father are committed to each other through thick and thin. A child without this security is at sea and has great difficulty developing that stability needed to cope with life and to build a lasting marriage later in life.

During the growing up years of our children we were separated for days at a time because of work and travel. We talked together about the separation. Numerous times before these out-of-town trips, one of our children developed high fevers which we could not understand. Finally the doctor diagnosed the problem as "daddyitis." This led us to take a different approach to such separations. We avoided any mention of Daddy's leaving beforehand and tried to spend special time together as a relaxed family.

A wise writer wrote words that we ought always to keep before us: "The massed experience of mankind would justify us in saying to any couple who sets out on the career of love, 'Now hold together. Hold together even when the light seems to have gone out, and your way looks dark and dull. Hold together even when it hurts.'"

Yes, if we were starting our marriage again, we would build on commitment, a commitment which is greater than any problem we face.

GARDEN OF LOVE

We shall walk together
in the garden of love
Where all the plants
of love, joy, and peace,
so much needed
for beauty and happiness,
are cultivated and nurtured;
Where all the flowers
of kindness, courtesy, and little remembrances
bloom and spread their fragrance
everywhere;
Where the trees blossom
and bear the rich fruit
of care and compassion
for which all life craves
and cannot exist without.

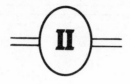

WE WOULD CONTINUE THE
COURTSHIP

William Jennings Bryan was posing for a portrait. The artist asked him, "Why do you wear your hair so long?"

Bryan replied, "When I was courting Mrs. Bryan, she objected to the way my ears stood out, and so to please her, I let my hair grow over them."

"But," said the artist, "that was many years ago. Don't you think you should have your hair cut now?"

"Why?" said Bryan in astonishment. "The romance is still going on!"

If we were starting our marriage over again we would seek to continue the courtship. Love that lasts is not the love that led us to the altar but the love expressed and experienced each day. If kindness, courtesy, consideration, and words and acts of love were necessary for the nurturing of love in courtship, then these same elements of love are just as necessary for the maturing and maintaining of love in marriage.

Further, we now know that when we put into practice even a few of the common courtesies and kindnesses we practiced before marriage, our marriage goes on gloriously. If the little gifts chosen with care, the kisses on meeting and leaving, and the words "I love you" and "I appreciate you" are carried from courtship into marriage, marriage does not grow dull. On the other hand, we realize that no matter how good our marriage was at the start, it will not blossom in beauty and blessing if we leave out the very things which build love in the first place. We have found that when we miss opportunities to show and share love, it fades and becomes difficult to feel.

Shakespeare wrote:

> They do not love
> that do not show their love.

We might add, we do not grow in love if we do not speak and share our love. Sometimes we need to learn to love all over again. We need to renew and continue the courtship.

Learn to Love Again

We have found that marriage has its ebb and flow. In every marriage there are times of special closeness as well as times of tension and distance. It is unreal to expect marriage to continue on one high emotional level, to be a continual panacea for our troubles. Real life is not like that. The important thing is to know how to deal with the lows as well as the highs. Too often we tend to be escapist, and when difficulty comes we think immediately about how to get out, rather than concentrating on how to cope with the situation. Life in the 80's tends to be geared toward evading every discomfort. There are pills to prevent every kind of pain. We have forgotten that pain can produce perception and courage as well as a caring and compassionate spirit.

In the low times of marriage we have found it possible to love all over again. That is because love is not a shot in the arm which, if we receive it, will guarantee living happily ever after. It is not a bolt of lightning out of the blue which hits us and then we have it forever. It is not an arrow which Cupid shoots and suddenly we have it. *Love is a learned response.*

In marriage counseling we see couples who tell us that there is nothing left in their marriage. They no longer have any feeling of love for each other—every drop of love is drained away, they say. The only alternative they see is divorce. And they want our sanction to separate.

To such couples we simply say, "You did love each other one time, didn't you?"

"Yes!" they reply. "We did love, but it's all over. Our love is dead."

"Then there is only one thing you can do," we tell them. (Here the couple expects us to say that the marriage is done and the only answer is a divorce.) Imagine their surprise when we say, "The only thing you can do is to learn to love all over again."

"Learn to love again?" they ask in shocked response. "How can we do that?"

"You learn to love again in exactly the same way you did it in the first place," we answer—by doing and saying and practicing those things which built love in the beginning. *Just continue the courtship.*

"Our marriage was on the rocks," wrote a woman. "I didn't love Robert. Then I began to ask, 'How would I act if I did love my husband?' I consciously began learning his likes and dislikes. I prepared his favorite dishes. I joined in his hobbies. I bought surprises to put in his lunch. I gave him my love on every occasion possible. Now I love him with all my heart.

"My greatest reward came the other day when our teenager said, 'Mom, I'm lucky.' 'Oh,' I replied. 'Why?' 'Because you and Dad love each other. You'd be surprised how many kids have parents who fight and quarrel most of the time.'"

Love is often as much the fruit of marriage as it is the root of marriage. George E. Sweazey writes in his book, *In Holy Marriage:*

Marriage is not the result of love, it is the opportunity to love. People marry so that they may find out what love is. It is not destiny that makes a person the one true love, it is life. It is the hardships that have been faced together. It is bending over sick beds and struggling over budgets; it is a thousand good-night kisses and good morning smiles; it is vacations at the seashore and conversations in the dark; it is growing reverence for each other which comes out of esteem and love.[1]

Children Reap the Benefits

Children are blessed by parents who are happy with each other and who demonstrate their love for each other. A friend of ours, a teacher in Canada, asked his class of first graders before Father's Day, "What is a dad and why do you love him?" Among the many intriguing responses was this one: "A dad is a father and a boyfriend, my mom's boyfriend. I love him because he hugs me and kisses me. My Mom likes my Daddy too."

Happy the child who has such a sense of love

---

[1]George E. Sweazey, *In Holy Marriage* (New York: Harper & Row), p. 29.

between father and mother. When this kind of love is present, the child will reap all its benefits and blessings. But when it is not known, seen, and felt, it is nearly impossible to make up for its absence in any way.

Psychiatrist Justin S. Green said: "In my twenty-five years of practice, I have yet to see a serious emotional problem in a child whose parents loved each other and whose love for the child was an outgrowth of their love for each other."

When we reflect back on our experiences of closeness we remember how much these affected all our relationships. Our children felt delight and our love for them when they sensed our love for each other as husband and wife. They loved to join hands in a walk, as we joined hands with each other. As they entered their teens they sometimes said, "Mother and Dad, we want you to go out this evening for a good time together. We'll take care of things here." And we sensed all over again that when they saw and felt our love for each other as their parents, they felt the warmth and wonder of it in their own spirits.

To this day our children remember in detail the time they said: "Dad, we have a plan. We want you to go to the upstairs phone and call mother in the kitchen. We want you to make a date with her for the sweetheart banquet next month." They still speak of the excitement they felt as they listened to the conversation between us and as they helped us choose what we should wear for the special occasion.

Fresh Discoveries

Yes, if we were starting our marriage again we would continue the courtship. As we did in our courtship, we would treat our relationship as the most important thing in our lives—one great adventure together. We now know that the time spent together in doing those things which express love are not lost times but moments which multiply all that's good in life.

We now know that when we have romantic fun we enrich our feelings of love. When we cultivate common interests and enjoy them together, they bind us in bonds of love. We now know that when our children see us as lovers, our relationship with them is at its best. We now know that only as our children see our deep love for each other can they understand the meaning of true love and the meaning of God's love later in life.

We now know that as we continue the courtship we are forever finding fresh discoveries in each other's lives and personalities—discoveries more delightful than diamonds and more valuable than pearls. No diamond can compare to the value of the sudden, fresh realization that we care deeply for each other. Sometimes this realization comes through a crisis experience.

A friend of ours shared with us how insecure he felt early in his marriage. He sometimes felt very unsure about his wife's love for him. Late one evening he was working in the basement with an arc welder. Suddenly the welder hit an electric wire which caused a loud noise and a flash of light, and all the electricity went off. In the dark, he rushed to the garage to check the fuse box.

When he returned he found his wife sitting on the basement steps weeping her heart out. She had run to the basement upon hearing the loud noise, found it dark, called her husband—and he did not answer her call. "At that moment," he said, "I did not doubt my wife's love for me. And I have not doubted it since that day."

No pearl is as precious as loving kindness, a compliment, a smile, a forgiving spirit or voluntary helpfulness. The happiest partner is not the one who married the best person but the one who is able to bring out the best in the person he or she married.

We feel good about ourselves when we are affirmed. So we feel good about our relationships when we affirm and compliment each other. We find that compliments such as "You look good in that suit" or "That dress really makes you look sharp" lead us to dress in the same outfit again and again. I feel good about myself when John says: "I'm glad you didn't let yourself get fat. You were the most attractive woman at the banquet tonight. Your eyes sparkle and your face lights up when you converse with people."

I can remember during a discouraging time in my work Betty gave me the boost I needed for a long time by saying, "John, I know that you don't realize the tremendous confidence I have in you and the great confidence a lot of people have in you." I needed that word of assurance. And who should be able to give it better than a loving wife or husband?

In our marriage, a compliment given at the right moment often kept us from discouragement and even despair.

We now know that when we commit ourselves to each other's happiness, we multiply happiness. When we commit ourselves to say and do loving things, we are blessed many times over. When we commit ourselves to respect each other, we make each other respectable. When we honor each other, we make each other honorable. And when we forget ourselves in love for each other, we make each other lovely.

TODAY'S ROAD

We shall walk together
today.
We were born for today—
not yesterday or tomorrow—
nor can we walk
another road another day.
We cannot choose
to walk with those gone before
or walk with those who shall follow.
Today we will take time
to walk together.
We will not lead each other
or follow
but walk beside,
hand in hand
together.

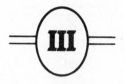

WE WOULD TAKE MORE TIME
TOGETHER

Love is spelled T I M E! Love is time together—to be with each other, to do things together and for each other, to relax together. Yes, if we were starting our marriage again, we would determine, from the start, to spend more definite, regular, planned-for time together.

We have been separated much over the years because of work which required travel. Many months we were separated more than half the time. When we were together we tried to build quality time, but that alone is not the answer. Special, regular times are needed to discuss specific concerns, especially what is bothering us. Unless we plan carefully, small things can become tremendous trifles which tear at our marriage. It is easy to become strangers even in the same family.

Some years ago we were separated for a long period of time. When we were reunited, we jotted down ten areas we felt we needed to discuss. These all had to do with our relationship as husband and wife. For several days we each wrote out what thoughts, concerns, or problems came to us concerning these areas. We told each other to write down not only what we were thinking but also what we were feeling, and to make as full a statement as possible for each of the ten areas. Then we took a day off by ourselves. We read to each other what we had written. After each subject we took time to discuss together our feelings, understandings, disagreements, and the adjustments we felt we needed to make. When we were satisfied we moved on to the next area.

We will never forget this experience, as well as other similar ones that have been valuable for clearing up our feelings about ourselves and each other.

We have also taken time to go for several days to a cabin in the mountains for renewal of our relationship. Our pattern here is to work together on projects or problems in the morning and then to walk hand in hand through the woods in the afternoon.

Before marriage we spent as much time together as possible. Somehow we knew our relationship could not grow or even exist, nor could our understanding of each other increase, without regular time together.

We discovered that after marriage a strange thing happens. We assume we are together and that we will be together always, and therefore we don't plan for time together. But this is not the case. After marriage we found that we tended to go our own ways. Often the only moments we have had together are those in which we are tired or irritated. The best time of the day is too often given to going elsewhere and doing things separately.

No wonder a marriage dries up. Marriage, a happy marriage, cannot exist on the crumbs or leftover scraps of time. A good marriage cannot develop on tired time (the time we get home, worn out). Meaningful communication, so essential to marriage, deteriorates when it is left for the hurried, late times. Without great care the prime time is taken over by the less important programs which will push their way into every marriage.

Further, love has a longing within itself to grow larger and more beautiful. Love does not remain the same. The love of the teens is different from the love of the twenties. And the love of the twenties is different from the love of the thirties. We are constantly changing, so we need time together to keep acquainted with our best friend. Being married and living in the same house does not guarantee anything. It certainly does not guarantee that we will not be lonely or that we will learn to know each other better. Some of the loneliest people we know are married people.

We learn to know each other and experience togetherness when we take the time to share each other's souls, to read each other's minds, and to enjoy each other's pleasures and presence.

Check Priorities

We have found that we must check our priorities again and again. What is most important? Our priorities shape and ultimately determine how we use our time, the persons with whom we use it, and the kind of benefits we expect to receive from it.

We have arrived at the point where we have three large categories we are sure of. The first claim upon our loyalty is God. When we put him first, we are blessed together. The second claim on our lives is family. And the third claim is our work.

Only when work is placed after family will family relationships be right and will our work, which in the final analysis depends so much upon how happy we are at home, be satisfying and successful. When work prospers and the family falls apart, work also suddenly loses its meaning.

Our marriage relationship, we believe, must be second only to our commitment to God. A dear friend said to us the other day: "One thing Jim has brought to our marriage is to put family before his work. He loves his work and has a lot to do but he knows when to lay his work aside and take time with me and the children. And that's great!" You know what else? Jim is also a great fellow at his job of teaching.

Jim can be great everywhere because he keeps his marriage in good repair. A man happy at his home makes a cheerful worker. And, since we know Jim and his family, we know also that they are persons who have time for all kinds of service to others. Somehow when family is in the proper place we have more time for God and also for work and service. Wayne Oates writes: "Surprisingly enough, finding time for each other ordinarily increases rather than decreases our efficiency at the very tasks that we use as excuses for not finding time."

We now know that if we are to have time together we need to *plan* time together. Each of us has the same number of hours in a week. Like a financial budget around which we plan our spending, we have a time budget around which we need to plan what is important.

Suppose we budget sixty hours for work and travel to and from work each week. Suppose we budget fifty-six hours for sleep. That still leaves us forty-two hours to spend on other things. How will we use those hours? Without some planning and thought, most of those hours will be wasted. Without careful planning we will spend those hours doing just about anything except being with our families. If we are to have time together—and love is spelled T I M E — we need to plan our time.

Beware of the Thieves

We must beware of the robbers who steal our time—robbers as real as any who might knock down the front door and steal our valuables. Television is a robber in the home. It robs us of precious hours of togetherness. Golf dates, all kinds of night meetings, sports events, and breakfast meetings can also steal time from the family. Since we plan for all of these, we can also decide to plan for time with each other.

Such planning is a sign that we have grown up and that we have outgrown adolescence—which is characterized by conforming to the pressures of the gang, friends, and outside activities. Part of growing up is realizing what takes second place to the greater commitment we have made to each other.

This may mean planning a meal away together each week. It may mean setting a definite time each day for some sharing. The secret is to find little bits of time regularly, rather than to wait for the big vacation or a whole free day in which to do something together. Even a half hour or less is better than nothing, and it is a lot less complicated and expensive than spending time later in a psychiatrist's or lawyer's office—which so often happens when couples do not take time together. We especially enjoy activities as simple as a mile-long walk around our neighborhood on a summer evening, or a drive into the country, or to a park. It's not only refreshing but is also a time when we can converse in private.

Several weeks ago we noticed the car was not working as it should. Because of our busyness we did not get it checked. We knew we would need to take it to the garage but kept putting it off. This morning the car did not start. Finally after a lot of time and work, we had the car taken to the garage and repaired. The trouble at the start was a simple thing which could have been remedied in a few minutes, had we seen to it immediately. Unattended to, it caused other mechanical problems, plus more time and inconvenience.

How like marriage this is. When we let little things go because we feel we don't have the time to talk about them and repair them, they become serious and affect our entire relationship. Because we don't take the time, major repairs are sometimes needed.

Before we were married we planned time together to do special things and go special places. And we planned time to just be together—alone. It is as we plan to do the same now in marriage that we find love growing in fresh and fulfilling ways. In addition, special times away, a day or two together, can also do wonders for relationships.

We need serious time periodically to talk about what is happening to us and to listen to the deep concerns each of us has. We need fun times together. The family or couple who does not have play times is missing out on many good memories.

We now know that the more time we take with each other, the more we cherish each other—as we make our moments together times of fun, caring, and conversation. An eastern college study reported that "nothing is more apt to smooth the course of love than communication: the level of marital satisfaction appeared to be related to the amount of time each day a couple spent talking together."

We now know that the guarding of regular times together makes times of separation precious in loving remembrance and longing for a speedy return.

Nourish the Family

Children are blessed when mother and father take time together. Children of all ages feel close to parents who have time for each other. You can see it in the little two-year-old who loves to snuggle between mother and father when they are sitting on the sofa. Children want their parents to express love for each other. As our children became older, they urged us to sit together rather than wanting to split us up.

Somehow both the smallest child and the growing adolescent feel parents have time for them if parents have time for each other, while the children who seldom see their parents in caring and sharing relationships feel estrangement and distance. It is always true that the way to build and nourish warm relationships with our children is to build them between ourselves.

One of the most inspiring times for our family is the togetherness we experience around the meal table. It is no surprise that the great dramatists of the ages put many of their great scenes around the table. Here is a great place of sharing in more than food.

When our children were young, we set aside Friday for family night. Since there was no school the next day, there was no homework to frustrate a leisurely, planned dinner hour. To make it more special, the children were not required to change clothes when they came home from school. The table was set in the dining room with our best table service, a tablecloth, and a nice centerpiece. The menu included something everyone enjoyed, and the dessert was eaten by candlelight.

Yes, if we were starting our marriage again we would plan, from the start, to spend more time together for our own sake, for our children's sake, and for heaven's sake.

COMMUNICATION

We shall walk together
with hands clasped and hearts united
until we feel each other's pulse,
until we do not fear to fall,
because we know we are sustained
by the strength of each other's hand,
by the courage of each other's heart
and by the comfort of each other's words.

We shall walk together
in silence—
until we sense speech stronger than words,
until we feel comfortable without words,
because we know the joy, strength, and support
of silence—
the inner oneness of soul,
the inner unity of spirit.

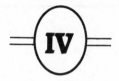

WE WOULD COVENANT TO
COMMUNICATE

"**W**e can't talk to each other."
"When we try to talk, we always get into a hassle."
"I can't reach him."
"She doesn't understand me."

All married couples have, no doubt, thought or used statements like these. In 90 percent of all marriage difficulties, communication is the major problem, and the difficulties in the other 10 percent are often directly or indirectly caused by the inability to communicate.

We realize this is true from our own experience. Also through counseling many married couples, and from the conclusions of numerous scientific studies, we are persuaded that if we were starting our marriage again we would, from the beginning, covenant to communicate.

As we look back over our experience, we realize now that when we got married we assumed we would communicate. After all, we longed for times to talk and share before marriage. We planned to do as many things together as possible before marriage. And we looked forward to marriage as a time when we could communicate without interruption as we learned to know each other more and more.

We assumed too much. Without a definite commitment to communicate, we became one of the statistics which say that in most marriages there is a decreasing ability to communicate after the wedding vows. Why? Not because we planned it that way. In fact, we realize that sometimes we failed to communicate because we didn't want to hurt the other, or we tried to ignore our feelings, thinking that our problems would go away.

However, problems do not disappear by our ignoring them. They only pile up and become inner irritations which build resentment and destroy love. Tiny trifles become tremendous vexations. Doubts grow in the shadows. Hiding our thoughts and feelings weakens the basic oneness of marital life. Only when there is openness and honesty can we experience healing, help, and happiness. Only as we share are "joys doubled and sorrows halved." Little things not dealt with multiply into unyielding giants which ruin relationships.

After our family included children our pattern of communication was changed. Each of us saw the other spending time with the children, so much so that a subtle jealousy crept in. But we both hesitated to mention it until a breakdown of communication caused us to notice what we were doing to each other. We needed to take some time off. Friends allowed us to use their cabin by the lake for a week. As we watched the children wade and make sand castles we were able to do some castle building ourselves.

Easy to Deal With

A joyful realization is that the problem of communication is one of the easiest problems to deal with—if we want to deal with it. There must first be the will to communicate. Then communication will happen. It may not happen right away. Outside help from a counselor may be needed to get communication started, but it will not be difficult if the desire is deep. Communication may need to start slow. At times it may be difficult and we may feel ill at ease, but the joy of sharing will grow and be worth every effort.

Certain elements are essential for effective commun-ication. It takes two to communicate. We must be aware of our own feelings. Each must express feelings without blaming or accusing the other. This allows the other to respond positively. Each needs to listen in order to understand. Each must empathize with the other until the feelings of the other are felt and understood.

We are created communicating creatures. And we are always communicating. Scientists estimate that 50 to 100 bits of information are exchanged each second between individuals communicating actively. Jackson and Lederer report, "Everything which a person does in relation to another is some form of message. There is no such thing as not communicating. Even silence is communication." Through word, gesture, touch, glance, raised eyebrows, tone of voice, a smile and silence, communication is sent and received.

We are made so that we desire to communicate. The verb *commune* means to share deeply our feelings and desires with trust and honesty. Each person longs to commune.

Different Levels

We learn to communicate at different levels. Sometimes we share only at the surface or cliché level—no more than "How are you today?" and "I like your dress." Other times we share only what we must to live in the same house: "If you are going to use the car you'll need to get gas." "If we are to meet that twelve o'clock appointment you'd better have the kids ready at eleven o'clock." "If I am to get groceries you'd better leave me some money." These kinds of conversations are those we must have if we want to exist together.

We may move a step beyond and share our thinking on different subjects. At this level we share what we have read in the newspaper or heard on the radio or TV. We share what the preacher said or what is going on in the community. We share who went to the hospital and who died or had a new baby.

While all these kinds of communication are important and necessary, meaningful marital communication starts when we share our deep inner feelings with each other in honesty and openness. Then we begin giving our real selves—the best gift we can give.

This deeper level of communication is difficult because it involves both risk and trust. How will my statements be taken? Will the other understand me? Will I be accepted after I bare my soul? We are told that teenagers will share with parents only to the point they feel they will still be loved and accepted. But that is true not only of teenagers, it is true of each of us. It takes trust to tell each other how we feel and what our needs are.

We have proven the truth of what Wallace Denton writes in *Family Problems and What to do About Them*: "Ten years from now you may not remember much of anything that I've said . . . but if you do remember anything, I want you to remember this: the degree to which your marriage succeeds or fails will be closely related to your ability to communicate with each other, to understand and be understood."

Lack of communication has caused all kinds of misunderstandings. One day after we had been married for some years, I simply said to Betty, without explanation, "Why don't you take care of the checkbook from now on?" Betty assumed responsibility for record keeping at that point without my realizing that she did it with some resentment.

Several years later we were participating in a marriage seminar when I shared how one marriage partner can do a job so much better than the other and in this way, if we recognize the gift of the other, we can complement each other. To illustrate I said: "Betty is a much better bookkeeper than I am, and so she keeps our checkbook. I was frustrated over the figures never coming out right, and she keeps it in perfect shape."

To my surprise, Betty spoke up and said, "Now you tell me! I always resented it that you told me to take care of the checkbook without any explanation. That clears the air." Numerous times Betty herself has used this as an illustration of how a short and clear explanation changed resentment into an understanding which makes the task enjoyable.

We now know the scripture statement—"Don't ever go to bed angry. If you do, you give the devil a chance to do his work" (paraphrased)—contains tremendous psychological and practical insight. We are a happy couple when we decide to discuss and settle differences and difficulties before going to sleep. If they are not dealt with and settled each day, they grow from little gnats which annoy into mighty monsters which destroy even the strongest love.

We shared this scripture and our experience in a seminar of married couples. Some months later, in an adjoining state, a couple came forward following a meeting. They asked, "Do you remember us? We were at your meeting (they named the place) and after the meeting we went home and covenanted together that we would never go to bed mad again. It has been the turning point in our marriage.

"We can usually tell," they continued, "when one of us is upset or angry about something. And so we say 'Out with it before we go to sleep!' It has transformed our marriage."

We have found it meaningful to take each other's hand as we are ready for sleep each night. Although there have been those very few times when we did not feel friendly enough toward each other to follow this routine, we cherish the practice and feel it is the final touch of love for the day.

Self-disclosure

We now believe in the importance of self-disclosure in communication. It is true, as modern communication experts say, that *love can only grow by fuller revelation.* Self-disclosure means the willingness to share who we are, our feelings and frustrations, delights and despairs, triumphs and temptations, pleasures and pains. This kind of sharing is the basis of all deep friendships. It is essential to all inner healing. It is the way to self-understanding and growth in love.

When the Bible refers to "one flesh" in talking about marriage, it is referring to more than our physical bodies. Becoming "one flesh" involves the unveiling of our inner selves. Then we begin giving to each other what we long for most—our real selves.

The level at which we communicate is the level at which we live. This does not mean that we are always talking.

We have learned that simply being together in the quietness of loving presence is a blessing, that the touch of the hand, the loving smile, the loving pat say "I love you" just as much as the words. We know that verbally and nonverbally we are always communicating in a positive or negative way. The quality of this communicating process is vitally important if we want to live together with creativity and with joy.

Lack of communication makes life very lonely. When we fail to share our feelings we find loneliness in ourselves and we become strangers to each other while living in the same house. When we fail to share our inner selves, life is lived on surface relationships which diminish real love.

On the other hand, when we share with each other, we feel appreciation for each other. When we put the needs of the other above our own, we feel fulfilled. When we agree together, even on small things, we sense a partnership.

We now know that in order to communicate, we need time. A study by a Hungarian sociologist, Karoly Varge, which included thirty thousand people in eleven countries, points out that the stability of marriage and the home depends upon the time spent talking together. The more time we take with each other, the more we look forward to times together. We need the fifteen minutes during the day, the little times to do something special together, and the more lengthy times for the revitalizing of our relationship and for the refreshing of our friendship.

A Place for Privacy

We realize the responsibility to give each other space and privacy also. We do not open each other's mail. We do not listen in on each other's telephone conversations. We do not check the contents of each other's pockets. Privacy rights in these and other areas can be acts of respect and good communication.

We have found that there are particular times of closeness and openness when it is more appropriate to raise deep feelings and differences. Some people have the uncanny knack of selecting the wrong moment to be completely honest. When a husband returns home tired after a difficult day at work, that is probably not the best time for a wife to tell him that she is very unhappy with the way the lawn looks or how dirty the garage is. When a wife has spent half a day getting ready for an evening out and is just ready to leave, it is probably a bad time to tell her she looks horrible in that particular dress. These kinds of comments can reveal hostility or aggression. Love, on the other hand, seeks to find special times of closeness and appropriate moments to discuss those things that disturb.

A communication breakdown between parent and child is usually preceded by a communication breakdown between father and mother. We have found that when our communication is open, honest, and loving, our child's willingness to share is strong. When the quality of communication between us as parents is poor, the less able our child is to objectively evaluate experiences and choices. Further, our child's experience in our home is the major preparation the child has for married life. This experience determines greatly the success of our child's own marriage. While our child may accept, modify, or reject our actions as parents, the understanding received about relationships in the family remains basic.

We have found that good communication is like a lubricant which keeps the wheels of our relationship running smoothly. The lack of good communication, however, is like sand in the gears of a fine machine.

Since real communication is the way to say "I love you," "I care for you," and "We are in this together," we would major in the art of communication if we were starting our marriage again. We would covenant to communicate.

BEYONDNESS

We shall walk together
in such service to each other
that serving will be perfect freedom;
in such care for each other
that caring will never be a burden;
in such giving to each other
that giving will never be a sacrifice;
in such living for each other
that life will overflow to all.

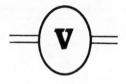

WE WOULD MAGNIFY ASSETS—
MINIMIZE LIABILITIES

In the wedding vows, both persons covenant "to bear with each other's infirmities and weaknesses." One of the best-known questions asked of those who marry is, "Do you take the person by your side for better and for worse?" The wedding vows are very realistic.

We found out soon after our wedding, if we had not faced up to it before, that each of us had (and still has) strengths and weaknesses. Each has a better and a worse side. And the "worse side" can be terribly unromantic, irritating, and sometimes downright unbearable. As so often happens we were attracted to our opposites. The rather shy person was attracted to the one who because of a good sense of humor was often the life of the party, one who felt comfortable in any situation. It was easy to join in the laughter and good times. Also it felt good afterwards as friends rehearsed the fun-filled evening together. It was a surprise to us to see how marriage made a switch. The outgoing one became irritated when the other was so quiet and had so little to share. When we came to the point that we understood that what irritated us was really a strength of the other person, we could begin to constructively deal with the difference.

If we were starting our marriage again, we would pledge immediately to seek to magnify the good qualities for which we chose each other and minimize the "worse" traits which tag along. This does not mean that we would not seek to improve and help each other overcome undesirable traits, but it does mean we would not allow these to become the center of attention and concern. After all, none of us changes until we feel loved and accepted as we are.

When we magnified each other's assets we began to see that the other, in spite of faults, was better than we imagined in qualities we needed and appreciated deeply. In his *Letters to Malcolm*, C. S. Lewis wrote: "Nothing which is at all times and in every way agreeable to us can have objective reality. It is the very nature of the real that it should have sharp corners and rough edges, that it should be resistant, should be itself. Dream furniture is the only kind on which you never stub your toes or bang your knee. You and I have both known happy marriage. But how different our wives were from the imaging mistress of our adolescent dreams. So much less exquisitely adopted to our wishes; and for that reason (among others) so incomparably better."

We Are Different Persons

We need to recognize that some traits we may consider the "worse" side, even a few months after marriage, will probably never change a great deal. For example, a talkative person usually chooses to marry a person who is more the silent type. After marriage the talkative one tries to turn the silent one into an outgoing conversationalist. Such a person will probably never become talkative. Forget it! We marry persons for the traits we ourselves do not have. Now our job is to learn to appreciate the traits, temperament, and characteristics the other has. If we do, we will see that these are exactly what we need to make us well-rounded persons.

Each partner has gifts and assets to contribute to the marriage, and the more these are recognized and respected, the happier the marriage. To marry an equal does not mean one of us cannot do things better than the other. A marriage is strengthened by receiving and encouraging the abilities of each. Studies show that in strong marriages spouses have learned to maximize each other's gifts. The more areas of respect and reception, the more satisfying the marriage.

It is best, we have learned, not to compare our marriage with others. Each person comes from a different background. Each person has different viewpoints on many things. "The goal of marriage," says Richard Dobbs, "is not to think alike, but to think together." Difference does not mean that one is better or worse than another.

In one marriage the wife takes care of servicing and cleaning the car and mowing the lawn. The husband takes care of the checkbook. This works well because of the interests and abilities of each. The opposite may be true in another marriage. We are happiest when we enable each other to do what each enjoys most and is most capable of doing. To compare one marriage with another, or to think that there are stereotyped rules, is to ruin relationships and to ignore abilities.

While special and separate gifts are apparent before

and immediately after marriage, other gifts and abilities are recognized after some time together. It took us some years to realize that one of us was a much better accountant than the other. Our marriage worked better when one assumed responsibility for our financial bookkeeping. The other enjoyed gardening and assumed responsibility there. In many other ways we can appreciate, enjoy, and profit from the differing gifts and interests of each other.

We must learn to appreciate differences in personality and perceptions. For a husband and wife to look at issues from different points of view can be a great help because it gives a broader perspective. When this fact is seen and experienced, partners build up each other rather than do battle with each other.

Marriage is a complementary relationship. *Complementary* suggests the blending of two distinct entities to make both better. And as we accept and appreciate what the other is, we become greater persons than we could ever be alone. Differences can drive us apart or add dimension, depending on how we approach them.

Learn to Affirm

We now know the enormous value of affirming each other in the intimate life of marriage. Affirmation is a basic cohesive factor in all happy marriage relationships. Too often we are like the old Vermont farmer who sat on his porch whittling while his wife sat beside him rocking and knitting. After a long, long silence the old man said, "You know, Sarah, you have meant so much to me that sometimes it's almost more'n I can stand not to tell you about it!"

Affirmation and praise cause love to flourish, just as water refreshes a beautiful flower.

We have learned that the drive to criticize usually reveals our own inadequacy, guilt, or jealousy. The ability to compliment, to appreciate, to accept, and to see the good in another reveals a secure person with inner peace, self-acceptance, and understanding. It also reveals a person who can admit failure and mistakes.

Few persons respond positively to negative criticism. Criticism may alter actions, but it is of no help in altering attitudes, which are far more basic. We are all inclined to become more caring, thoughtful, and generous, and the person we long to be, when someone notices and encourages our good qualities.

Affirmation and Children

So, when we encourage and appreciate our spouse we are not only making that person a greater person, we are also building our own self-worth and strengthening the relationships so important to marital happiness.

The same is also true in relation to our children. The child who is constantly criticized becomes critical. But, even more, the child becomes unsure, insecure, attacking others in many ways and developing little self-esteem. It's when we as parents magnify the assets and minimize the liabilities of the child that the child develops self-confidence and learns the qualities of graciousness and acceptance so basic to all of life. Here again, we see the close relationship of behavior practiced between husband and wife to the pattern we develop with and for our children.

Some time ago we shared in a delightful wedding.

Near the close of the ceremony, the bride and groom asked those in attendance for advice as they began their marriage journey. They said, "Some of you have been married a long time. You have learned what is important for a successful and happy marriage. We are now starting out. What advice do you have for us?" After a short silence persons began to share. Among the numerous significant suggestions was one given by a grandmother. "I believe your marriage will be happy," she said, "if, each day, you share one thing you appreciate about the other."

We agree. If we were starting our marriage over again we would seek to magnify each other's good points and minimize the infirmities and weaknesses.

REMINDED

We shall walk together
in such tenderness and truth
that, though we walk separate paths,
even the trifles of each day
and night
may remind us
of the love and trust
each holds for the other
and deepen the desire
to come together again—
soon.

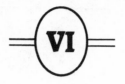

WE WOULD REVEL IN THE
GOODNESS AND BEAUTY OF SEX

Is sex important in married life? Of course, it is very important. It is one of the elements which hold a marriage together and make it satisfying. Sex can also be that element which tears an unsatisfactory marriage apart. But sex is not the *most* important element. It is a sensitive thermometer telling the temperature of the marriage.

That last statement is the opposite of what most of us have been led to believe. It is stressed by many books, articles, advertisements, TV, and movies that sex is the keystone of marital success and happiness. The impression is given that, if sexual intercourse is good, the marriage will be good.

We disagree. In fact, we take an opposite viewpoint. Our experience is that when marriage is good, caring, and loving, sex is good. And if love is not expressed in the other relationships of marriage, sex becomes hollow, empty, and unsatisfactory.

Yes, sex is significant in each marriage. It is meant to be good and satisfying and emotionally nourishing. Sex is highly desirable and delightful, but our sexual experience serves rather to reveal the condition of the rest of our relationships than to determine those relationships. When other parts of the relationship in marriage are good, sex is satisfying; when the relationships in marriage are poor, sex is unsatisfactory.

One of the reasons we married each other was because we were attracted to each other physically. And one of the reasons we are still attracted to each other is that we find each other sexually attractive and satisfying. We believe sex is good not only because the Bible proclaims it, but because we acclaim it to be good. However, we have learned that real sex is quite different from that portrayed by "reel" sex (what you see in movies, television, and magazines). Real sex is much more and far better than a few moments of erotic, forbidden pleasure. Sexual union is but one of a complicated set of relationships and activities which make up the whole interactional pattern of marriage. How we talk to and treat each other in the kitchen and living room determines our response in the bedroom.

Sexual Success

The search for sexual success is a mania today. But what is sexual success? We must be aware that for many people the "standards" of sex are set by advertisers, by the infidelity portrayed in soap operas, by neurotic literature, movies, plays, and television. And these standards are filled with fantasy, falsehood, and infidelity. We dare not develop our standards from these if sex is to be meaningful.

We must also realize that much of the information about sex comes from so-called experts who report expressions and experiences of people with unsatisfactory experiences, sick marriages, and illicit relationships outside the realm of fidelity, caring love, and Christian commitment.

This stress on the negative or illicit aspects of sex takes attention away from what needs to be the primary focus if sexual relationships are to have real meaning, pleasure, and fulfillment. The primary focus must always be on a loving relationship in other areas of life if sexual intercourse is to have pleasure and purpose and to be all God intends it to be.

In his fine book *Whom God Hath Joined*, David R. Mace writes: "We often talk about sexual intercourse as 'making love.' Strictly speaking, that is not true. The meeting of two bodies cannot make love. It can only express and enrich a love that is already there. And the quality of the experience will depend upon the quality of the love that it expresses."[1]

So we have found that when things go wrong with sex, the problem is not sex. Sex is God's good gift. Problems with sex come when we do not deal with our other problems.

Unity Expressed in Sex

Our sexual experiences as husband and wife reveal more about our relationships in other areas than anything else we do. The unity we sense in sexual intimacy stems from how united we are in other things. Our openness and honesty in sexual relations tell how open and honest we are in the rest of our life together. The communication of our feelings in sex is closely related to the kind of communication we experience in all of marriage.

Also, the love we feel in sexual intercourse flows

---

[1]David R. Mace, *Whom God Hath Joined* (Philadelphia: Westminster Press, 1973), p. 53.

from the love we express and feel throughout the day. The joy we experience in this most intimate of relationships is the result of the joy we find in the presence of each other at other times. And the satisfaction of sexual intimacy corresponds to the satisfaction we experience as partners in all of life.

Therefore if we desire a sense of oneness, openness, communication, trust, and feelings of love, joy, and satisfaction in sexual intercourse, we must practice bringing all these qualities to all our relationships as husband and wife. Sexual intimacy will then heighten and confirm these qualities.

Further, life's purpose for married partners is not all passion and ecstasy. Most of marriage is made up of the mundane chores of every day. So the only way to live happy lives is to invest the common tasks with quality. Then they will become sources and expressions of sexual intimacy.

Good and to Be Enjoyed

If we were starting our marriage again we would keep in mind that sex is God's creation and is good, pure, right, and to be enjoyed in the marriage relationship. So sex should be spoken about together freely and frankly until all attitudes of hesitancy and fear, shame and guilt are gone. Otherwise relationships suffer. We would seek to invest sexual relations with all the pleasure possible and to do and say those things which make them the most pleasurable for each other.

If we were starting our marriage again we would realize that sex is one of the primary ways we express our love for each other and meet each other's needs. Therefore, it is a grave mistake to withhold sex for any wrong motives such as to retaliate against or to control the other. That kind of withholding only brings serious repercussions; it builds hostility and tears a marriage into shreds.

Scripture is surprisingly clear also in this. "The husband should give to his wife her conjugal rights, and likewise the wife to her husband . . . Do not refuse one another except perhaps by agreement for a season, that you may devote yourselves to prayer; but then come together again, lest Satan tempt you through lack of self control" (I Corinthians 7:3, 5 RSV).

The point is plain. We should not withhold sexual love from each other. Although differences can be exaggerated, sex can be more important for one spouse than the other. One may have stronger sexual urges and needs. To withhold sexual relations can place that spouse under severe temptation to unfaithfulness.

In order to achieve understanding and satisfaction open communication is needed. Feelings and needs should be shared. Partners need freedom to tell what it is that gives pleasure and what hinders sexual fulfillment. The greater the freedom to express love, feelings, and needs, the greater the satisfaction and joy.

Patience and Practice

We have learned that first efforts at sexual intercourse are seldom skillful or satisfying. Statistics say that less than 50 percent of people experience initial satisfaction. For 10 percent it may take twenty years or more. But even then, when love, honesty, and concern are present, there is an inner sense of pleasure and oneness.

No duet is perfect at its first practice, but with patience and practice harmony is realized. So it is with the experience of sex. On the other hand, no amount of factual knowledge can bring lasting satisfaction if we do not bring love to the act.

We have learned that satisfying sex depends more upon such virtues as kindness, courtesy, openness, and consideration, than upon skill or knowledge. When we approach the sex experience with the attitude of giving happiness and pleasure, and seeking to meet the needs of the other, we find joy returned and our own needs met. When both find fulfillment, renewal, and uplift, sex is good and the bonds of unity and love are strengthened.

One writer defines sexual intimacy without inter-personal intimacy as the equivalent of a diploma without an education—an apparent achievement with no real substance behind it. How can we express love in bed if we do not take the time to cultivate the expressions of love outside of bed? The loving kiss, word, hug, or touch during the day does as much to add to the delight of sexual union.

Therefore a loving relationship seeks the satisfaction of the loved one. A caring relationship seeks the welfare of the other. A truthful and trustful relationship allows each the freedom to share fully what produces the most pleasure and what hinders enjoyment. The overall attribute is love. As Harry Stack Sullivan said years ago: "When the satisfaction or the security of another person becomes as significant to one as one's own satisfaction or security, then a state of love exists."

Dare Not Be Ignored

We have learned that the sexual area of married love is one which cannot be ignored if marriage is to be happy. In other areas of married life there can be disagreement and yet a couple can live happily. Here, because the very biological urge brings us together, we must either deal with our problems and differences or settle for an unsatisfactory sexual and marriage experience.

We have learned that we dare not leave this important love expression to be crowded into the hours of fatigue or hurried moments. Sex, to be enjoyed, needs plenty of time, when a couple can relax in each other's arms. It is easy to become so occupied with living that we leave no time for loving.

Sex has a special, individual meaning for each couple. If we give love and accept love, sex falls into its proper perspective. Sexual intimacy is fed by love and feeds love. A real part of married bliss is to know the exhilarating joy of sexual love.

THROUGH DIFFICULTIES

Though the walk ahead
be full of falls,
let it be said
that we did not fail
to lift one another up again.
Let it be said
that our faults seemed few
because our eyes
did not expect perfection
and our minds
did not dwell on weakness.
Let it be said
that we multiplied our joys
because we shared them,
and that our love grew large
because we gave it away.

VII

WE WOULD STOP TRYING TO
CHANGE EACH OTHER

After the honeymoon, the new husband asked his bride, "Dear, you don't mind if I point out a few little faults you have, do you?"

"Absolutely not," replied the young wife. "It's those little faults which kept me from getting a better husband, dear."

"What have you learned these days together?" we asked a group of couples at the final session of a marriage enrichment seminar. A wife, with tears in her eyes, had an immediate response. "What I have learned is that I must stop trying to change Bill. I've tried for twenty-five years to change him. And it hasn't worked one bit. I see what I need to do is to love him and accept him."

If this wife learned that lesson, she was well on the way to a happy marriage. Her husband, sitting by her side, was a fine person, loved by all of us there. Yet they had struggled for years because, in this instance, the wife sought to change rather than love and accept.

One of the early and chief temptations in a marriage is for one or both partners to seek to become Creator all over again and try to create the other into his or her own image. Sometimes the struggle starts in court-ship. Sometimes it starts soon after the wedding vows. But whenever we try to change each other we are headed for hostility, trouble, and reaction. Then the opposite sex becomes the opposition sex. When we try to change each other, rather than accept each other, we say, "You are unsatisfactory." When we feel pressure to change, we respond with resistance and dig in our heels. So married life becomes an endless duel rather than an enjoyable duet.

An area where we've had as many hard feelings and difficulties as any in our marriage is getting to places on time. Early we learned that one of us is a prompt person while the other is not as time conscious. Again and again this built ill-feelings at the very time we should have been feeling especially good toward each other. To head for a church service to speak of love or to start out to conduct a husband-wife retreat when we were angry with each other because we'd left late again was not conducive to anything good.

We've worked hard at this one and, in the main, have succeeded in reducing this kind of friction a great deal. We decided we have too many meetings to open and too many schedules to keep to let such a habit handicap us. We decided to work at it together, helping each other so we can get ready in good time and planning ahead in order to avoid the mad rush.

We Marry Persons We Need

We choose to marry a person because of who and what that person is. We pick a person to marry with traits we appreciate and which complement ours. Even though we may never consciously think about it, we tend to choose a companion for life who has the opposite abilities and temperament to ours because we need that which we ourselves do not have. A talkative person marries a quiet person; an extrovert marries an introvert; a person who is prompt marries one who finds it difficult to be on time anywhere; a person who likes to go to bed early and get up in the morning marries one who likes to stay up late at night and has difficulty getting up in the morning; the person who is meticulous about details marries one who is interested in the broad issues; the practical person marries the sentimentalist; a realist marries a dreamer; a person who must analyze everything marries a person who jumps into things without scrutiny.

On and on we could go illustrating how we choose persons to marry who are our polar opposites. Why? Because we are weak where the other's strength lies. We choose one to marry who has traits we lack and which we admire. The problem is that after the wedding we find our mates unacceptable where they are different. Then we set out to make the person over into our likeness.

We do and say many things which tell the other that he or she is not acceptable. We say things like, "You are just like your mother," or "My dad always helped around the house." In a hundred ways we tell each other how unacceptable the other is. Yet most battles in marriage are battles over the very things for which we chose each other in the first place!

We have found that it never pays to try to change each other. Our job is not to change but to love and accept the other. The Scripture says, "Accept one another, even as Christ accepts you." And when we love and accept then all kinds of possibilities for change are opened up. In fact it is only when we feel loved and accepted the way we are that we are motivated to change.

With our children the same thing is true. The child who does not feel loved and accepted is a child who will react and resist. The child who feels love and acceptance responds with readiness to what he or she senses the parent wishes.

Expectations Are Too High

Part of our problem can also be that our expectations and demands on each other are very high. The expectations range from material, sexual, and financial ones to psychological and religious ones. Further, our expectations of the physical and psychological rewards of marriage and family life are growing far more rapidly than our capacities to deal with the challenges and problems of human intimacy.

A generation ago the expectations for marriage were not much more than settling down, eking out an economic existence, having a number of children, and enjoying life together.

Today expectations of all kinds are pushed at the married couple, which, if we buy them, cannot possibly be met by anyone, and therefore can produce frustration. Who can measure up to being always the most beautiful, best dressed, best educated, most able at sex, always agreeable and understanding possessor of the neatest and best-behaved kids, and in the fifty-thousand-dollar income bracket?

Even mannerisms or habits that pass unnoticed in friends and casual acquaintances often assume importance out of proportion and provoke extreme annoyance when practiced by our partner. The happiest couple is the one which can preserve a sense of proportion about the relative importance of events and actions.

Often we expect a perfection of each other that only God can meet. Reuel L. Howe, in *Sex And Religion Today*, writes: "Much marriage difficulty and unhappiness are due to the failure of the partners to accept the fact of their finiteness and its meaning. Instead, they hold themselves up to ideas of performance possible only to God." Fulton J. Sheen also cites expectations we have as unreasonable. He writes: "Too many married people expect their partner to give that which only God can give, namely, an eternal ecstasy." Yes, we have learned, at least to some degree, that it is good to accept each other's finiteness.

If we were starting our marriage again we would more than ever seek to admit our own failures and finiteness and be more tolerant of each other. When we see ourselves as fallible, vulnerable human beings we can accept each other's shortcomings in love and in spite of failure.

Look for the Best

To look for the best we need to overlook a lot in each other and recognize that we all have plenty of faults. The important thing is not that we have faults but what we do with them.

A dear friend of ours was talking about the conversation in a women's group which had met in her home. It seemed that the subject was husbands, and one negative remark after another was brought up. Finally she said, "The way it sounds, you are trying to get rid of your husbands. Land sakes! I'm doing all I can to keep mine!" Might her attitude be the reason she and her husband have such a good relationship?

If we were starting our marriage over again we would determine to live and to love the real partner we have, not the imaginary partner we dreamed about. We have learned that it never works out when we try to be a missionary to our spouse. Frankly there is something arrogant about trying to make a person into something that he or she is not. Sometimes it may seem impossible to survive the idiosyncrasies of our partner. But we can if we will, and it is easier than surviving the resistance which results from trying to change the other.

One wife described her difficult and unhappy days when she was demanding, nagging, and complaining. The reason she was so annoyed by her husband, she said, was that she was thinking of herself too much. But with God's help and strength she changed and developed what she calls a "4-A Strategy: accept him, admire him, adapt to him, appreciate him." The formula will work for a husband too!

We have learned that criticism seldom, if ever, helps. To express, at times, how the other's behavior makes us feel, without labeling or lambasting the other, may be helpful. But the personal attack can only cut and leave scars in our relationships.

We have learned that a sense of humor helps. When we can laugh at ourselves, we are on the way to a relaxed relationship, and can avoid the up-tight type of living which causes friction and sparks whenever we touch.

We have learned that it is good to forgive and to cultivate a good forgetter.

> The kindest and the happiest pair
> Will find occasion to forbear;
> And something, every day they live,
> To pity, and perhaps forgive.

William Cowper

Yes, after all the years of marriage, we believe that learning to love and accept each other is one of the biggest jobs we have—one which also carries some of the richest rewards.

FAITHFUL IN LITTLE THINGS

We will walk together
with the persistent prayer
for God to make us larger
in little things,
and to grant us eyes
eager to see
the small things of every day
which enlarge life,
which add gladness,
which fill life full of radiance,
so that above all else
we may be found faithful
in little things.

WE WOULD BE GREAT IN
LITTLE THINGS

Friends of ours had a TV which was not working. They turned the dials and checked the fuse box. One of them even gave it a kick, thinking that a jar might flick it on. Finally the repairman was called. In no time he noticed that someone had pulled the cord out of the electric socket! No one had thought of checking that!

"Always in repairing anything," the repairman told the family, "check the small and simple things first. Ninety-nine percent of troubles are with the small things."

We have found it's the little things which make or break a marriage. Most of us can manage enough muscle to handle the major things in life such as accidents, financial failure, and even death. When a marriage fails it is because partners failed to practice the little kindnesses and to speak the little words of love. Little acts and words of love add luster and joy to life, whereas their absence causes coldness to creep in. The small neglects of love in time can become a tremendous collection of trifles which can tear two lovers apart.

Therefore our prayer each day must be, "Lord, make us great in little things." For it is the little things which wear the garments of greatness. The small things of life make us glad or sad.

What We Remember

As we reflect on our marriage today, we cannot think of many big things which we did. We do remember the encouraging words we said to each other during times of discouragement, the times we relaxed together by heading to some quiet place, and the cards and small gifts we gave at unexpected times.

In our family we have a cup called "the family cup." We searched a long time for it. Finally a dear friend, who knew we were looking for such a cup, found one and gave it to us. It is a tall, communion-like cup. We do not use it at all as a regular cup. Rather, in a ceremony it becomes a simple symbol of our family unity. When our family passes the cup around the table, each child and parent drinks from it and then shares a special word of love and appreciation for the others, it enlarges our love. Passing the cup is a small symbolic act, but it is great in building a loving and caring relationship and in creating a sense of unity.

We remember the joining of hands around the table as we prayed for one another and thanked God for His blessings. We remember the walks in the woods or the stroll hand in hand in the evening sunset. We remember the touch of love while driving along in the car. We remember the prayers we prayed in the car before leaving on a trip, prayers for the safety of others and ourselves as we traveled and for a happy time together. All these are little things which loom large in the storehouse of our family memories.

If we were starting our marriage again we would put much more stress on such little things. As we think back we know it is the little things we remember most. The little words "please" and "thank you" carry great reward. "I'm sorry,""excuse me," and "let me help you" are like love songs set to beautiful music and can be performed by all. And while great brilliance, beauty, and intellect can be admired, they cannot dry a tear or mend a broken spirit. Only kindness can do this.

William Hordern explains why telegraph and cable companies spell out punctuation marks instead of using symbols such as commas, periods, and question marks. A lady touring Europe cabled her husband: "Have found wonderful bracelet. Price seventy-five-thousand dollars. May I buy it?"

Her husband promptly cabled back, "No, price too high." The telegraph operator in transmitting the message missed the signal for the comma. So the wife read the message, "No price too high." She bought the bracelet. Her husband sued the company and won.

A comma is such a small thing that it seems insignificant. But it illustrates the truth that small things can make much difference in life. And most of life is made up of small things.

Transferred Treasures

Today we know that a little word of appreciation makes the whole day blossom into a day of delight. Without a sense of appreciation even our best efforts become drudgery. Today we know that a touch of tenderness can turn a mournful morning into a melody of gladness. Without tenderness life grows tough. Today we know that a little help with some chore can make the meanest task a labor of lasting love. Without a spirit of helpfulness life grows lonely and turns to drudgery.

Today we know that when we take a little time for each other, all our time is transformed into treasured moments. Today we know that if marriage is to have meaning and joyful togetherness, it will be because of faithfulness in the small things and not because we waited for the big occasion or opportunity to demonstrate devotion to each other.

It is true as the Scripture says, "The one who is faithful in a very little is faithful also in much; and he who is dishonest in a very little is dishonest also in much" (Luke 16:10 RSV).

Disaster Is Not Sudden

When a marriage suffers seemingly sudden failure it is really not something which is sudden. Beneath the surface for a long time, partners did not practice faithfulness in the small things.

Robert E. Goodrich in his book *What's It All About?* illustrated the working of a hurricane. A hurricane is an evil, death-dealing, monstrous thing. But how does a hurricane work its destruction and death? You will notice, in the news descriptions, statements similar to this: "The hurricane was preceded by torrential rains." This is the secret strategy of a hurricane.

Rain precedes the wind by a number of hours. Millions of tiny raindrops soften the earth. When everything is softened, suddenly the wind strikes. And the giant trees which could easily stand the storm under normal circumstances are pushed over. Houses and buildings which could have stood much stronger winds suddenly give way because the soil was softened.

So the hurricane is a parable. When marriages fail, the failure is preceded by many small things done or left undone, which cause a deterioration in the soil and which are needed to build strong relationships. Then along comes some kind of adversity or difficulty and the marriage is destroyed.

Impact on Children

Little acts and words of love demonstrated in the daily life between husband and wife speak loudest of the nature of real love to our children. Some time ago, our daughter wrote expressing the warm family feeling of love she had when she saw the fresh rose her father had brought in before breakfast from the garden for her mother on a summer morning. This was not a big thing, to be sure. But it was a little gift of love. Yet the fragrance of love and feelings of love between father and mother reach out to bless all the family and beyond.

Likewise it is the little things we do and say to our children which set the stage for relationships and love. If as parents we wait for the special occasions, the big trips, and the "When I have time to play a game" to demonstrate love, we will find life passing us by, and even these special times will lack a real sense of love. Also the multitude of other opportunities to show and experience love are missed.

If we were starting our marriage again we would seek to major in the little things. We would not wait until we had a lot of time or money to take a trip together. We would take a short stroll in the park or join in some other activity together. We would not plan only for special times together, when vacation time comes around, but we would seek to make many moments of family time special by seeing how we could make mundane moments of every day special.

We would not wait for the occasional days such as birthdays and anniversaries and Christmas to express our love and to tell each other we are glad God led us together. Yes, we would tell each other then. But more, we would seek to invest many other occasions with the time and effort which say, "You are important to me."

M. A. Kelty wrote: "Small kindnesses, small courtesies, small considerations habitually practiced in our social intercourse, give greater charm to the character than the display of great talents and accomplishments."

Julia Carney wrote the familiar words:

> Little deeds of kindness,
> Little words of love
> Help to make earth happy
> Like the heaven above.

We have found that when we failed in the little things of life, we missed the big opportunities to prove our faithfulness. When we failed to show love in the little things, we found it more difficult to celebrate the big occasions. When we failed to express appreciation in the small things and little words, our effort at the big things sounded hollow.

So we are persuaded, more than ever, that the way to great love, appreciation, and faithfulness, as well as a growing oneness, is the practice of love and appreciation faithfully in the small things of every day.

GOD THE GIVER

We shall walk together
knowing that all life
is a gift from God
and that he has made us
his caretakers
of all he gives.
We shall remember
that all the things of life
are not so much ours
as they are God's,
given to bring blessing
as we are faithful stewards
and conscious always
that real, enduring life
cannot be found in anything
which does not last
beyond time.

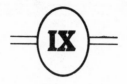

WE WOULD COVENANT ON
FINANCES

Some months after our marriage a salesman stopped at our door. While he presented his
product, we each imagined the other liked the item
and was interested in purchasing it. We bought it.
After the salesman left we soon learned our mistake.
Neither of us really wanted it enough to make the
purchase. Nevertheless, we had signed on the line. As
we think of it now, though it was not a large item, the
experience taught us a good lesson. Out of it we made
an agreement. We would not purchase anything that
cost over $50 and that was unplanned for without first
discussing it and agreeing on it.

That decision has saved us from many unnecessary
purchases and much misunderstanding over the
years.

Money Reveals Us

If we were starting our marriage again we would
covenant together regarding our use of money. The
way we earn, spend, give, and save our money is a

revelation of our philosophy of life and, of course, determines the kind of life-style we will live.

money is not everything in life. However, the way we handle money reveals rather accurately what we are and what we are becoming. A good question for us to answer is, What kind of life do we want to live? And we should not stop thinking about it until we are satisfied with the answer.

Studies show that over 50 percent of married couples have severe struggles over finances. Money is an emotional subject. Next to communication and scheduling time in marriage, the money problem is the big one. We need to be purposeful in our use of money. What life-style do we desire? What debts can we stand? What will be our buying patterns? What level of giving is planned? Will credit cards be used? How much should be saved?

Life Is Not Material

If we were beginning our marriage again we would stress the fact that a good marriage does not depend upon material things—a bigger and more beautiful house, a new car, or the latest in clothes.

A husband and wife who were separated when they came for counsel said it was after they built their third house—and each one was bigger and better than the last—that they found their marriage was headed for the rocks. Many persons consciously or unconsciously decide for money and mansions over marriage, and are forever unhappy. The Bible says, "Better a meal of vegetables where there is love than a fatted calf with hatred" (Proverbs 15:17 NIV).

We would beware of the trap of installment buying. Business and industry employ some of the best psychologists in the world to package, portray, and place products to persuade people to buy. No one is paid to persuade the public to develop sales-resistance to things not needed.

Robert Hastings points out that money management is not so much a technique as it is an attitude. Attitudes deal with emotions. So managing money is controlling one's emotions. If we are to control money we must learn to control ourselves. Undisciplined use of money usually reveals undisciplined persons.

Dewitt L. Miller, in *If Two Are to Become One*, writes: "It is also worth noting that a couple who keeps an accurate accounting of the way their money is spent will, in almost every instance, spend less and spend more wisely than a couple that keeps no accounts."[1]

Money, like fire, is a faithful servant but can be an awful danger. Because of this we must master it. A couple can do much in relieving undue pressures on marriage by sound agreements.

We have learned that it is good to agree to live within our income. No one can long spend beyond one's income and get away with it. And the size of the income has little bearing on family financial frustration and fights. The problem is the attitude we have toward money. The obvious fact, sometimes hard to learn, is that any marriage gets in trouble soon if partners spend more than they take in.

We have learned that the more open we are as a family on finances, the more cooperation and understanding we experience. Children should also share in this concern and be held responsible for helping make ends meet.

---

[1] Dewitt L. Miller, *If Two Are to Be One* (Elgin, Ill.: Brethren Press, 1960), p. 63.

From the start of our marriage, as pastor and wife our income was low. But we did several things we are very happy about today. Not only did we practice giving at least a tithe to God's work but we taught our children to tithe from the first dime they received. In addition, as the children turned twelve, we gave them a small allowance out of which they bought their own clothes. We helped out at birthdays and Christmas with larger items such as coats or shoes, but the children learned if they exceeded their allowance, the extra spending was coming out of their future earnings. This practice proved a tremendous training in teaching them to buy and select wisely and to realize their responsibility for choices. We would do this again.

One teenager griped continually because he felt his parents were stingy, did not buy him clothes and other things the way his friends' parents did for their children. After the parents sat down with him and explained their income and the family budget, the young man responded, "I didn't know you had to think of all those things. You are sure good managers."

A plan of spending on which the family agrees is needed for a happy home. Agreed on, it will not do if only one partner carefully follows the plan while the other splurges beyond the agreement.

A Review Is in Order

We have learned that it is good to review finances—income and spending as well as saving and giving—from time to time. If this is not done, an excellent plan may fail because income may diminish, costs of certain items may change radically, and family needs continually change as children are born and grow older. Circumstances change over the years.

We have found that usually one spouse is much better able to handle finances than the other. So we have agreed as to who shall take charge of the check-book in our home. Many times the wife is more suited by temperament and ability to keep the family economy on a good basis and keep the check-book balanced. Regardless of which one does it, the important thing is to seek openness and honesty and the welfare of all.

We have found that when money becomes the place of battle, the problems in our relationship are probably elsewhere. Money can simply be an excuse for releasing stored up resentments. However it can also be a means for creating great joy and growing commitment as we reach out to each other in using material things to bless marriage. We can use money to be masters over each other, or masters over ourselves in letting it provide an important opportunity for pulling together in marriage.

Although some may consider the following figures unrealistic, they may give some guidance from which to work. A financial counselor who has helped many families over the years suggests that a couple probably should not spend more than two and a half years' income for a house. A couple should aim to accumulate half a year's income in a reserve fund and should move toward providing two years' income in life insurance or pension funds. Borrowing should be done wisely and only on income-producing or cost-saving items. Diversify assets. Save some money each year, and don't miss the blessing of taking out what you plan to give to charity.

We have found real satisfaction in our marriage by understanding and openness in finances, and if we were starting our marriage again we would covenant together regarding our use of material resources.

IN GOD'S PATHS

We shall walk together
on the pleasant paths
prepared by God himself.
Then each step
shall bring us closer to him
and to each other.
We shall join hands
in such service
that we shall never
walk alone.
We shall join in prayer
until the petitions of our hearts
beat as one
with God and with each other.
We shall walk together
with such love
for eternal values
that everywhere we move,
life's lasting possessions,
of love, joy, and peace,
will be ours—
making their home
wherever we are together.

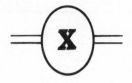

WE WOULD KEEP THE TRIANGLE STRONG

George MacDonald, the Scottish writer of a century ago, said to his wife, "My dearest, when I love God more, I love you the way you ought to be loved." We know this is true.

Our relation to God has been left for last in this little volume not because it is the least important of the subjects, but because it is foundational and undergirds all the others.

We picture our relationship as a triangle with God at the top. The closer each of us comes to God, the closer we come to each other.

At the wedding of Princess Elizabeth and Phillip, Geoffrey Francis Fisher, Archbishop of Canterbury, told the royal couple: "The ever-living Christ is here to bless you. The nearer you keep to Him, the nearer you will be to the other."

We have found this is true. We entered marriage believing that God led us together and that our commitment was first to him and secondly to each other. And we've experienced happiness and meaning in our marriage in proportion to our adherence to this perspective.

This desire to serve God faithfully and our common Christian commitment have helped us in choosing the places we have served, in using our money, and in conducting our interpersonal relationships. Certainly we failed time and again, and our priorities were not always as clear as they ought to have been; but our basic commitment helped us work through failures and find forgiveness and faith again and again.

We also know many marriages which have experienced new life or have moved from the mediocre to the meaningful by placing God in his proper place.

A Sacred Covenant

A good marriage is not so much a contract between two persons as a sacred covenant between three—God, wife, and husband. If we are not committed to honor God, there is not much we can do to resist the overwhelming degradation and destruction of marriage today.

Hazen G. Werner wrote: "Family love and understanding are made complete when God is there. The lives of all members of the family depend on the ultimate good, life with God."

If we were beginning our marriage again, we would seek to keep the triangle strong. We would covenant with each other, from the start, to put into practice those attitudes and actions which place God at the center of our home.

Like most Christian couples, we assumed that, after marriage, prayer and Bible reading would come naturally and be a part of daily experience. Like many other couples, however, we soon realized that our being Christians does not cause these practices to happen automatically. And, although we regularly prayed before each meal and at other times, we know it was less than we desired.

We found also that there were times we missed prayer and Bible reading together for one reason or another. We skipped them because our schedule was switched or because of poor planning and what we thought was lack of time. Yet we knew we were missing the greatest blessings promised to even two people who will ask anything in the name of Jesus. The precious promise of God's answer when two people pray is not only for persons at a church prayer meeting but for the husband and wife who will covenant together in prayer.

Today we know that it is not only possible to claim and receive God's promise as a married couple, but it is also a responsibility and a privilege given us by our Lord. It is one of the great gifts of marriage to pray as a couple. And yet it is a gift often unclaimed by married people.

Why Neglect?

Why are the privileges of prayer and reading God's Word unclaimed? They are unclaimed because of neglect. We neglect them because we do not plan for them to be as much a part of our lives as eating and work. We neglect them because they require honesty. We cannot have wrong relationships and pray with meaning and reality. This is why the Bible warns us not to have a spirit of bitterness against a spouse. Such a spirit hinders prayer.

Why else is the privilege of prayer and Scripture reading unclaimed? It is because a God-centered life is not consistent with the values of power, money, and self-gratification perpetuated by our culture. A selfish spirit and the spirit of Christ are contrary one to the other.

We know that to make marriage work we need the God who created us and pronounced marriage good. A marriage needs forgiveness, and God makes forgiveness possible. A marriage needs grace, which means that we receive more good things than we deserve, and God makes us gracious, giving persons. A marriage needs mercy, which means that judgment is withheld when we deserve to be punished. And God gives us mercy for ourselves and for each other.

We know that a marriage needs the broader fellowship of God's people. If there is to be a firm faith it must include fellowship with God's family, the church. Many factors prove this is true. In North America more than two marriages in four will end in divorce. Yet studies show, over the years, that of those who are active and committed to a local church the likelihood of divorce is closer to one in five hundred.

God knows we need, especially today, a body of persons to help and encourage us in the right way, in the midst of those elements everywhere which tear marriage apart.

For Stability and Strength

While we know that going to church, praying and reading the Bible together will not guarantee a successful marital relationship, we know also the tremendous stability each of these gives to our marriage. Whenever we strengthen these ties and practices, our lives are enlarged. Love for these, God's gifts to us, enriches all our relationships. We know from experience that faithfulness in these areas bears the fruit of love, joy, and peace.

We are more sure today than ever that God led us together, because he continues to lead us in a thousand ways. In seeking his guidance together, and following his way, we are doubly assured that we are in his will. We have the witness of each other.

We know the privilege of praying together about plans and needs in our own lives and in behalf of others. We know the joy of sharing together God's power. We do not feel alone in our spiritual walk because we know the support we share when we are together as well as when we are absent. All this is God's gift to those who keep the triangle strong.

We have learned in our walk with God that to live and love does not mean merely to look into each other's eyes. It means also to look out together, to serve beyond ourselves, to lift the loads of others, and to help meet the needs of those next to us and beyond. Some of the most unhappy people are those seeking happiness only for themselves. In contrast, the most meaningful and happy moments in marriage are those in which we join hands in prayer and work for the blessing of others.

No two persons can live only for each other. Life's meaning begins to become clearer when we look out in the same direction to serve in a cause greater than ourselves.

In his article "Christian Marriage: A New Vocation" Orin N. Hutchinson, Jr. says:

Marriage becomes more than just a couple's coming together to meet each other's needs and to seek mutual enjoyment. From the Christian perspective, it becomes a covenant. The two covenant to become a part of God's work in the world, a part of God's purpose for this time and place and day, the means through which God's caring and helpfulness and service reach out to life everywhere.

Some marriages get into difficulty because the marriage has become an end in itself. When that happens, we put more expectations on marriage than marriage can carry. But from the Christian perspective, marriage can become a means to an end. The end is bigger than the marriage: What difference can the two of you make in the life of the world? Whom can you help? What caring can you bring? What causes serve?[1]

This too is the way our children become useful persons in our world. Only as they sense selfless living can they absorb a spirit of selflessness. Thus our homes become spiritual launching platforms from which we send our children out to serve the world.

Yes, we find that when we are close to God, we are close to each other. When we are close to each other it is easy to make contact with God. If we were starting out in marriage, we would seek to keep the triangle strong.

---

[1] Orin N. Hutchinson, "Christian Marriage: A New Vocation," p. 9. Reprinted with permission from *The Christian Home*, June-August, 1982. Copyright © 1982 by The Upper Room.

IN JOY

We shall walk together
in joy—
the joy of old memories
and new beginnings,
of old truths
and new faith,
of past pleasures
and dreamed-of pursuits.

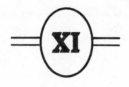

WE WOULD REALIZE IT'S
NEVER TOO LATE

No marriage is completely unique. Marriage problems are very similar. And success or failure depends more on how we deal with our problems than on the fact that we have them.

In our thirty-plus years of marriage we have needed to begin again and again. There were times when communication seemed to be meaningless and at a standstill. We talked only about those things we needed to talk about to live in the same house. At times we felt lonely and unloved. At times we wondered about our love and whether we might be happier had we married someone else. During the difficult times of child-rearing and the disappointments which have come when children stray, we felt the strain which resulted from placing blame on each other.

In spite of all of these experiences we know that even the most difficult things in life can be doors to new beginnings, understandings, and growth in greater love than we ever imagined at the start of our marriage.

In many areas of life we are past the place of beginning again. When children are grown and gone it is impossible to begin again to raise and nurture them. We have contributed as much as we can to their growing up years; now our major contribution is to stand by and be available when they need us. This inability to correct past mistakes and to do it over brings sadness to every parent to one degree or another. What parent has not said, "If I had it to do over I would do it differently"?

But marriage is different. As long as we have breath there is the possibility of beginning again. We can still put all these short chapters into practice. Any marriage can be changed and improved if there is the will to change and improve. We need not settle down, satisfied with a static or unsatisfactory relationship.

William J. Lederer and Don D. Jackson, in *Mirages Of Marriage*, write:

> Somehow, a myth has arisen in this country which teaches that the first few years of marriage form the period during which all problems get ironed out. The implication seems to be that thereafter the spouses sit passively while the marital wagon rolls along through life. This conception of the relationship is nonsense . . . Divorce figures indicate how fallacious this myth really is. Interviews with hundreds of couples clearly show that those who resign themselves to a static relationship are inviting divorce, desertion, or disaster. Disaster comes in many forms in marriage, from psychosomatic and mental illness all the way to the grim life of the Gruesome Twosome.[1]

Change Is Always Possible

The happy marriage is made by those who believe that change is always possible and that life is always

[1]William J. Lederer and Don D. Jackson, *The Mirages of Marriage* (New York: W. W. Norton, 1968), p. 199.

improvable. In the happy marriage there is the will to change and to expand the perception of our needs and feelings. And in the happy marriage, spouses learn to adjust and yield in order to develop those relationships which add vitality and meaning to life.

André Maurois quoted in *The Art of Living*, "A successful marriage is an edifice that must be rebuilt every day." One can look at such building of marriage as drudgery and undesirable toil. Those who see marriage in this light have not yet caught the vision of the joy of working together and the beautiful dwelling God intends marriage to be.

We would rather say that marriage is an edifice which we are building every day. We decide the beauty of the building we live in. When we look at it this way we see that we are building for each other the kind of house we will live in. Sometimes we may realize that part of the structure is weak and needs strengthening. At other times we may need to do remodeling to make the house more useful, safe, and serviceable. At times we notice repairs are needed if the house is not to crumble. All these actions are necessary in marriage.

But, in addition, a builder knows the joy of designing something beautiful which is a pleasure to live in. He sees the possibilities of placing a window at just the right place so the vistas of the mountains, the valleys, the sunrise and sunset can be enjoyed. All this is the possibility of marriage.

Like a Beautiful House

Certainly there will be repairs needed in every marriage. Change also is a law of life. But there is the excitement of building something beautiful which is a